POWER ROUTINES IV

A 30 Day Guided Tour of the
Habits of Gratitude, Scripture Reading, Journaling and Prayer

By Chuck Allen
AChuckAllen.com
@AChuckAllen

POWER ROUTINES IV
A 30 Day Guided Tour of the
Habits of Gratitude, Scripture Reading, Journaling and Prayer

Formatting and layout by
Andy Smith
andrew@sugarhillchurch.com

Cover design by
Ethan Hyma
ethan@sugarhillchurch.com

Welcome to Power Routines IV

Nothing has encouraged and sharpened more than building the habits of Gratitude, Scripture Reading, Guided Journaling and Specific Prayer. These four disciplines have now become a part of my morning routine, or better said, my **POWER ROUTINE!**

When I get intentional about my attitude of gratitude, I am setting myself up for a great day. When my attitude is set on being grateful, all that I have is more than enough! Gratitude is a powerful emotion that can set the course for success. It dares your attitudes to reflect on the glass half full and the best in life. Starting the day with gratitude has become an essential part of my day. Regardless of what is going on, I am eager to answer the question, "What am I grateful for today?" It has made me far more pleasant, productive, fulfilled and happy. I am positively confident that the same will be true for you!

I've always read the Bible, but through Power Routines, I've learned that the key to getting Scripture into my life isn't about quantity but quality. I want to challenge you to read Scripture with one desired outcome - TO KNOW GOD MORE FULLY. I read the Bible every day, not with a desire to check off a task list, but instead with an intentional desire for God's Word to get inside my heart and my head and transform me into the person and leader God desires me to be. If we are to have a "renewing of our mind," we must invest in saturating our mind with God's Word.

Journaling is simple for some but a challenge for most. To stare at an empty page and ponder what to write can be a daunting task but that's why Power Routines asks you three simple questions. All you need to do is answer the questions and you will unlock the power of capturing your thoughts, lessons learned and relational capital. Journaling has improved my awareness, creativity and relationships to the degree that I will journal daily for the rest of my life. The key to journaling is to write whatever the truth is to the question asked. It is for you, not for public display. As a result, you can answer in bullets, sentences or paragraphs. You pick! I promise you that this simple habit will strengthen you in every facet of your life.

Right after the three question journal section is a declaration. It is designed for you to set your focus for each day. My daily declaration is a statement of intent. It's the what I am and will be today statement!

Then there is Guided Prayer and Meditation. It is exactly as it sounds. Building this discipline into your life will absolutely draw you into a closer relationship with the Divine. This is the one Power Routine that also includes an audio sibling, weekdaymeditation.com. First, list who you are praying for and why. Then, list what you are praying for. And then, list answers to prayers that you see, experience and believe. Once done, listen to the Weekday Meditation and let me walk you through a guided prayer and a short time of quietude and solitude. Don't miss this powerful guided meditation!

The number one question that I am asked about Power Routines is this, "How do you practically do this every day?" It's simple- here is my typical morning routine:

- Gratitude: What three things am I grateful for right now? (2 minutes)
- Read Scripture (3 minutes)
- Journal- Answer three questions. (2 minutes)
- Declaration- One brief but powerful statement about your day (1 minute)
- Pray and Meditate- This includes listening and praying with the Weekday Meditation. (7 minutes)

If you are counting, that's about fifteen minutes. You can accomplish all of this in more or less time, but know this, it's not a race, it's a habit. Habits are best created when we start small and add as we find benefit. I have no doubt that you will find great benefit from developing these POWER ROUTINES!

That seems simple enough, right? Just fifteen minutes each day and you can build a spiritual POWER ROUTINE into your life!

Let's Do This!

Chuck Allen

*"When you are grateful for what you have,
what you have is more than enough"*

⚡ **GRATITUDE |** Today, I am grateful for...

A good nights sleep

Payday is today

My family is healthy

"Feed your soul with God's truth"

⚡ **SCRIPTURE**

1 Timothy 1:3-4
When I left for Macedonia, I urged you to stay there in Ephesus and stop those whose teaching is contrary to the truth. Don't let them waste their time in endless discussion of myths and spiritual pedigrees. These things only lead to meaningless speculations, which don't help people live a life of faith in God.

⚡ **SCRIPTURE**

2 Timothy 1:3-4
Timothy, I thank God for you—the God I serve with a clear conscience, just as my ancestors did. Night and day I constantly remember you in my prayers. I long to see you again, for I remember your tears as we parted. And I will be filled with joy when we are together again.

What is the Lord speaking into your life through these verses?

I must not wast time with false teachings.

What did you learn about the Lord?

God has a clear conscience.

"For whom, what and why am I praying today?"

⚡ **Prayer |** Who am I burdened for today?

Who? _Barbra_   Why? _Cancer_

Who? _Mark_   Why? _Tough Divorce_

Who? _Lisa_   Why? _Finances_

What? _That John does well in his new job._

What? _____

Praise: _Thank you Jesus for my health._

⚡ **Prayer |** What else needs prayer?

Our country and the world

_____

_____

⚡ **Answered Prayer |** A good time for gratitude

Mike has recovered from his surgery.

My uncle was able to sell his house.

_____

_____

_____

"Capture the essence of the last 24 hours"

⚡ **Journal |** What lessons did I learn?

I need to listen more and talk less.

⚡ **Journal |** Today will be successful if...

Get my work done and get to spend time with family.

⚡ **Journal |** Declaration: Today I will...

Today I will quick to listen and slow to speak.

**WANT TO FILL YOUR DAY WITH
A CUP OF ENCOURAGEMENT?**
Experience the Weekday Podcast
WeekdayPodcast.com
5 minutes a day and 5 days a week

⚡ **Journal |** Things I'm excited about

My wife comes home from vacation!

⚡ **Journal |** Yesterday's Wins and Challenges

My work presentation went well!
It was hard for me to get out of bed.

Jesus is all that I need in
my life. I will have bad days
but He will always be by my
side. The Lord will protect
me and He has blessed me
with all that I have. God
chose us by sending His son
to die for us and He will
always be for us.

Additional Thoughts?

Each life is made up of
mistakes and learning,
waiting and growing,
practicing patience and
being persistent.
-Billy Graham

*"When you are grateful for what you have,
what you have is more than enough"*

⚡ **GRATITUDE** | Today, I am grateful for...

_____

_____

_____

"Feed your soul with God's truth"

⚡ **SCRIPTURE**

1 Timothy 1:3-4
*When I left for Macedonia, I urged you to stay there in
Ephesus and stop those whose teaching is contrary to
the truth. Don't let them waste their time in endless
discussion of myths and spiritual pedigrees. These
things only lead to meaningless speculations, which
don't help people live a life of faith in God.*

⚡ **SCRIPTURE**

2 Timothy 1:3-4
*Timothy, I thank God for you—the God I serve with a clear
conscience, just as my ancestors did. Night and day I
constantly remember you in my prayers. I long to see you
again, for I remember your tears as we parted. And I will be
filled with joy when we are together again.*

What is the Lord speaking into your life through these verses?

_____

_____

What did you learn about the Lord?

_____

_____

*"For whom, what and why am
I praying today?"*

⚡ **Prayer |** Who am I burdened for today?

Who? _____ Why? _____

Who? _____ Why? _____

Who? _____ Why? _____

What? _____

What? _____

Praise: _____

⚡ **Prayer |** What else needs prayer?

_____

_____

_____

⚡ **Answered Prayer |** A good time for graditude

_____

_____

_____

_____

_____

"Capture the essence of the last 24 hours"

⚡ **Journal** | What lessons did I learn?

_____

_____

_____

_____

⚡ **Journal** | Today will be successful if...

_____

_____

_____

_____

⚡ **Journal** | Declaration: Today I will...

_____

_____

_____

_____

**WANT TO FILL YOUR DAY WITH
A CUP OF ENCOURAGEMENT?**
Experience the Weekday Podcast
WeekdayPodcast.com
5 minutes a day and 5 days a week

⚡ **Journal** | Things I'm excited about

_____
_____
_____
_____

⚡ **Journal** | Yesterday's Wins and Challenges

_____
_____
_____
_____

Additional Thoughts?

_____
_____
_____

Each life is made up of
mistakes and learning,
waiting and growing,
practicing patience and
being persistent.
-Billy Graham

_____
_____
_____
_____
_____
_____

*"When you are grateful for what you have,
what you have is more than enough"*

⚡ GRATITUDE | Today, I am grateful for...

_____

_____

_____

"Feed your soul with God's truth"

⚡ SCRIPTURE

1 Timothy 1:8-9
*We know that the law is good when used correctly.
For the law was not intended for people who do what is
right. It is for people who are lawless and rebellious,
who are ungodly and sinful, who consider nothing sacred
and defile what is holy, who kill their father or mother or
commit other murders.*

⚡ SCRIPTURE

2 Timothy 1:5-7
*I remember your genuine faith, for you share the faith
that first filled your grandmother Lois and your mother,
Eunice. And I know that same faith continues strong
in you. This is why I remind you to fan into flames the
spiritual gift God gave you when I laid my hands on you.
For God has not given us a spirit of fear and timidity, but
of power, love, and self-discipline.*

What is the Lord speaking into your life through these verses?

_____

_____

What did you learn about the Lord?

_____

_____

"For whom, what and why am I praying today?"

⚡ **Prayer** | Who am I burdened for today?

Who? _____ Why? _____

Who? _____ Why? _____

Who? _____ Why? _____

What? _____

What? _____

Praise: _____

⚡ **Prayer** | What else needs prayer?

_____

_____

_____

⚡ **Answered Prayer** | A good time for graditude

_____

_____

_____

_____

_____

"Capture the essence of the last 24 hours"

⚡ **Journal** | What lessons did I learn?

_____

_____

_____

_____

⚡ **Journal** | Today will be successful if...

_____

_____

_____

_____

⚡ **Journal** | Declaration: Today I will...

_____

_____

_____

_____

Discover Peace, Power, & Direction
ON THE WEEKDAY MEDITATION
Meditative prayer guided by Pastor Chuck Allen
WeekdayMeditation.com

⚡ **Journal** | Things I'm excited about

_____

_____

_____

_____

⚡ **Journal** | Yesterday's Wins and Challenges

_____

_____

_____

_____

Additional Thoughts?

_____

_____

_____

_____

_____

Prayer is simply a
two-way conversation
between you and God.
-Billy Graham

_____

_____

_____

_____

*"When you are grateful for what you have,
what you have is more than enough"*

⚡ **GRATITUDE** | Today, I am grateful for...

_____

_____

_____

"Feed your soul with God's truth"

⚡ **SCRIPTURE**

1 Timothy 1:12-14
*I thank Christ Jesus our Lord, who has given me
strength to do his work. He considered me trustworthy
and appointed me to serve him, even though I used
to blaspheme the name of Christ. In my insolence, I
persecuted his people. But God had mercy on me because
I did it in ignorance and unbelief. Oh, how generous and
gracious our Lord was! He filled me with the faith and
love that come from Christ Jesus.*

⚡ **SCRIPTURE**

2 Timothy 1:8-9
*So never be ashamed to tell others about our Lord.
And don't be ashamed of me, either, even though I'm
in prison for him. With the strength God gives you, be
ready to suffer with me for the sake of the Good News.
For God saved us and called us to live a holy life. He
did this, not because we deserved it, but because that
was his plan from before the beginning of time—to
show us his grace through Christ Jesus.*

What is the Lord speaking into your life through these verses?

_____

_____

What did you learn about the Lord?

_____

_____

*"For whom, what and why am
I praying today?"*

⚡ **Prayer** | Who am I burdened for today?

Who? _____   Why? _____

Who? _____   Why? _____

Who? _____   Why? _____

What? _____

What? _____

Praise: _____

⚡ **Prayer** | What else needs prayer?

_____

_____

_____

⚡ **Answered Prayer** | A good time for graditude

_____

_____

_____

_____

_____

Journal | What lessons did I learn?

_____

_____

_____

_____

Journal | Today will be successful if...

_____

_____

_____

_____

Journal | Declaration: Today I will...

_____

_____

_____

_____

4ForFriday
Recommended Reads, Listens, Learnings,
and Reviews every Friday
from achuckallen.com

⚡ Journal | Things I'm excited about

_____

_____

_____

_____

⚡ Journal | Yesterday's Wins and Challenges

_____

_____

_____

_____

Additional Thoughts?

_____

_____

_____

_____

_____
I believe that the
greatest form of prayer
is praise to God.
-Billy Graham

_____

_____

_____

_____

_____

*"When you are grateful for what you have,
what you have is more than enough"*

⚡ **GRATITUDE** | Today, I am grateful for...

_____

_____

_____

"Feed your soul with God's truth"

⚡ **SCRIPTURE**

1 Timothy 1:15-17
*This is a trustworthy saying, and everyone should accept it:
"Christ Jesus came into the world to save sinners"—and I
am the worst of them all. But God had mercy on me so that
Christ Jesus could use me as a prime example of his great
patience with even the worst sinners. Then others will realize
that they, too, can believe in him and receive eternal life. All
honor and glory to God forever and ever! He is the eternal
King, the unseen one who never dies; he alone is God. Amen.*

⚡ **SCRIPTURE**

2 Timothy 1:10-11
*And now he has made all of this plain to us by the appearing
of Christ Jesus, our Savior. He broke the power of death and
illuminated the way to life and immortality through the
Good News. And God chose me to be a preacher, an apostle,
and a teacher of this Good News.*

What is the Lord speaking into your life through these verses?

_____

_____

What did you learn about the Lord?

_____

_____

"For whom, what and why am I praying today?"

⚡ Prayer | Who am I burdened for today?

Who? _____ Why? _____

Who? _____ Why? _____

Who? _____ Why? _____

What? _____

What? _____

Praise: _____

⚡ Prayer | What else needs prayer?

_____

_____

_____

⚡ Answered Prayer | A good time for gratitude

_____

_____

_____

_____

_____

"Capture the essence of the last 24 hours"

⚡ **Journal** | What lessons did I learn?

_____

_____

_____

_____

⚡ **Journal** | Today will be successful if...

_____

_____

_____

_____

⚡ **Journal** | Declaration: Today I will...

_____

_____

_____

_____

INSTIGATING BETTER BLOG
FRESH THOUGHTS ON
LIFE AND LEADERSHIP
at achuckallen.com

Journal | Things I'm excited about

_____

_____

_____

_____

Journal | Yesterday's Wins and Challenges

_____

_____

_____

_____

Additional Thoughts?

_____

_____

_____

_____

God proved His love on the
Cross. When Christ hung,
and bled, and died, it was
God saying to the world,
'I love you.'
-Billy Graham

_____

_____

_____

_____

_____

_____

*"When you are grateful for what you have,
what you have is more than enough"*

⚡ **GRATITUDE** | Today, I am grateful for...

_____

_____

_____

"Feed your soul with God's truth"

⚡ **SCRIPTURE**

1 Timothy 1:18-19
*Timothy, my son, here are my instructions for
you, based on the prophetic words spoken about
you earlier. May they help you fight well in the
Lord's battles. Cling to your faith in Christ, and
keep your conscience clear. For some people
have deliberately violated their consciences; as a
result, their faith has been shipwrecked.*

⚡ **SCRIPTURE**

2 Timothy 1:12
*That is why I am suffering here in prison. But I am
not ashamed of it, for I know the one in whom I
trust, and I am sure that he is able to guard what
I have entrusted to him until the day of his return.*

What is the Lord speaking into your life through these verses?

_____

_____

What did you learn about the Lord?

_____

_____

"For whom, what and why am I praying today?"

⚡ **Prayer |** Who am I burdened for today?

Who? _____ Why? _____

Who? _____ Why? _____

Who? _____ Why? _____

What? _____

What? _____

Praise: _____

⚡ **Prayer |** What else needs prayer?

_____

_____

_____

⚡ **Answered Prayer |** A good time for gratitude

_____

_____

_____

_____

_____

"Capture the essence of the last 24 hours"

⚡ **Journal** | What lessons did I learn?

_____

_____

_____

_____

⚡ **Journal** | Today will be successful if...

_____

_____

_____

_____

⚡ **Journal** | Declaration: Today I will...

_____

_____

_____

_____

PASTOR'S BOOK CLUB
PURPOSEFUL, MEANINGFUL READS
from Pastor Chuck Allen
achuckallen.com

⚡ **Journal** | Things I'm excited about

_____

_____

_____

_____

⚡ **Journal** | Yesterday's Wins and Challenges

_____

_____

_____

_____

Additional Thoughts?

_____

_____

_____

_____

The wonderful news is that
our Lord is a God of mercy,
_____   and He responds
to repentance.
-Billy Graham
_____

_____

_____

_____

*"When you are grateful for what you have,
what you have is more than enough"*

⚡ **GRATITUDE** | Today, I am grateful for...

_____

_____

_____

"Feed your soul with God's truth"

⚡ **SCRIPTURE**

1 Timothy 2:1-4
*I urge you, first of all, to pray for all people. Ask God to
help them; intercede on their behalf, and give thanks
for them. Pray this way for kings and all who are in
authority so that we can live peaceful and quiet lives
marked by godliness and dignity. This is good and
pleases God our Savior, who wants everyone to be
saved and to understand the truth.*

⚡ **SCRIPTURE**

2 Timothy 1:13-14
*Hold on to the pattern of wholesome teaching you
learned from me—a pattern shaped by the faith and
love that you have in Christ Jesus. Through the power
of the Holy Spirit who lives within us, carefully guard
the precious truth that has been entrusted to you.*

What is the Lord speaking into your life through these verses?

_____

_____

What did you learn about the Lord?

_____

_____

"For whom, what and why am I praying today?"

⚡ Prayer | Who am I burdened for today?

Who? _____ Why? _____

Who? _____ Why? _____

Who? _____ Why? _____

What? _____

What? _____

Praise: _____

⚡ Prayer | What else needs prayer?

_____

_____

_____

⚡ Answered Prayer | A good time for graditude

_____

_____

_____

_____

_____

⚡ **Journal** | What lessons did I learn?

_____

_____

_____

_____

⚡ **Journal** | Today will be successful if...

_____

_____

_____

_____

⚡ **Journal** | Declaration: Today I will...

_____

_____

_____

_____

THE WEEKDAY
PODCAST

**WANT TO FILL YOUR DAY WITH
A CUP OF ENCOURAGEMENT?**
Experience the Weekday Podcast
WeekdayPodcast.com
5 minutes a day and 5 days a week

⚡ **Journal** | Things I'm excited about

_____

_____

_____

_____

⚡ **Journal** | Yesterday's Wins and Challenges

_____

_____

_____

_____

Additional Thoughts?

_____

_____

_____

_____

God's mercy and grace
give me hope - for myself,
and for our world.
-Billy Graham

_____

_____

_____

_____

_____

*"When you are grateful for what you have,
what you have is more than enough"*

⚡ **GRATITUDE** | Today, I am grateful for...

_____

_____

_____

"Feed your soul with God's truth"

⚡ **SCRIPTURE**

1 Timothy 2:5-7
*For, There is one God and one Mediator who can
reconcile God and humanity—the man Christ
Jesus. He gave his life to purchase freedom for
everyone. This is the message God gave to the
world at just the right time. And I have been
chosen as a preacher and apostle to teach the
Gentiles this message about faith and truth. I'm
not exaggerating—just telling the truth.*

⚡ **SCRIPTURE**

2 Timothy 1:16-18
*May the Lord show special kindness to
Onesiphorus and all his family because he
often visited and encouraged me. He was never
ashamed of me because I was in chains. When
he came to Rome, he searched everywhere until
he found me. May the Lord show him special
kindness on the day of Christ's return. And you
know very well how helpful he was in Ephesus.*

What is the Lord speaking into your life through these verses?

_____

_____

What did you learn about the Lord?

_____

_____

"For whom, what and why am I praying today?"

⚡ **Prayer |** Who am I burdened for today?

Who? _____ Why? _____

Who? _____ Why? _____

Who? _____ Why? _____

What? _____

What? _____

Praise: _____

⚡ **Prayer |** What else needs prayer?

_____

_____

_____

⚡ **Answered Prayer |** A good time for graditude

_____

_____

_____

_____

_____

"Capture the essence of the last 24 hours"

⚡ **Journal** | What lessons did I learn?

_____

_____

_____

_____

⚡ **Journal** | Today will be successful if...

_____

_____

_____

_____

⚡ **Journal** | Declaration: Today I will...

_____

_____

_____

_____

Discover Peace, Power, & Direction
ON THE WEEKDAY MEDITATION
Meditative prayer guided by Pastor Chuck Allen
WeekdayMeditation.com

⚡ Journal | Things I'm excited about

_____

_____

_____

_____

⚡ Journal | Yesterday's Wins and Challenges

_____

_____

_____

_____

Additional Thoughts?

_____

_____

_____

_____

_____

My home is in Heaven.
I'm just traveling
through this world.
-Billy Graham

_____

_____

_____

_____

_____

"When you are grateful for what you have, what you have is more than enough"

⚡ **GRATITUDE** | Today, I am grateful for...

_____

_____

_____

"Feed your soul with God's truth"

⚡ **SCRIPTURE**

1 Timothy 2:8
In every place of worship, I want men to pray with holy hands lifted up to God, free from anger and controversy.

⚡ **SCRIPTURE**

2 Timothy 2:1-2
Timothy, my dear son, be strong through the grace that God gives you in Christ Jesus. You have heard me teach things that have been confirmed by many reliable witnesses. Now teach these truths to other trustworthy people who will be able to pass them on to others.

What is the Lord speaking into your life through these verses?

_____

_____

What did you learn about the Lord?

_____

_____

⚡ Prayer | Who am I burdened for today?

Who? _____ Why? _____

Who? _____ Why? _____

Who? _____ Why? _____

What? _____

What? _____

Praise: _____

⚡ Prayer | What else needs prayer?

_____

_____

_____

⚡ Answered Prayer | A good time for graditude

_____

_____

_____

_____

_____

"Capture the essence of the last 24 hours"

⚡ **Journal |** What lessons did I learn?

_____

_____

_____

_____

⚡ **Journal |** Today will be successful if...

_____

_____

_____

_____

⚡ **Journal |** Declaration: Today I will...

_____

_____

_____

_____

4ForFriday
Recommended Reads, Listens, Learnings,
and Reviews every Friday
from achuckallen.com

⚡ Journal | Things I'm excited about

_____

_____

_____

_____

⚡ Journal | Yesterday's Wins and Challenges

_____

_____

_____

_____

Additional Thoughts?

_____

_____

_____

_____

Man has two great
spiritual needs. One
is for forgiveness. The
other is for goodness.
-Billy Graham

_____

_____

_____

_____

_____

_____

*"When you are grateful for what you have,
what you have is more than enough"*

⚡ **GRATITUDE** | Today, I am grateful for...

_____

_____

_____

"Feed your soul with God's truth"

⚡ **SCRIPTURE**

1 Timothy 3:1-2
*This is a trustworthy saying: "If someone aspires to
be a church leader, he desires an honorable position."
So a church leader must be a man whose life is above
reproach. He must be faithful to his wife. He must
exercise self-control, live wisely, and have a good
reputation. He must enjoy having guests in his home,
and he must be able to teach.*

⚡ **SCRIPTURE**

2 Timothy 2:3-4
*Endure suffering along with me, as a good soldier
of Christ Jesus. Soldiers don't get tied up in the
affairs of civilian life, for then they cannot please
the officer who enlisted them.*

What is the Lord speaking into your life through these verses?

_____

_____

What did you learn about the Lord?

_____

_____

"For whom, what and why am I praying today?"

⚡ **Prayer |** Who am I burdened for today?

Who? _____ Why? _____

Who? _____ Why? _____

Who? _____ Why? _____

What? _____

What? _____

Praise: _____

⚡ **Prayer |** What else needs prayer?

_____

_____

_____

⚡ **Answered Prayer |** A good time for graditude

_____

_____

_____

_____

_____

"Capture the essence of the last 24 hours"

⚡ **Journal** | What lessons did I learn?

_____

_____

_____

_____

⚡ **Journal** | Today will be successful if...

_____

_____

_____

_____

⚡ **Journal** | Declaration: Today I will...

_____

_____

_____

_____

INSTIGATING BETTER BLOG
FRESH THOUGHTS ON
LIFE AND LEADERSHIP
at achuckallen.com

⚡ Journal | Things I'm excited about

_____

_____

_____

_____

⚡ Journal | Yesterday's Wins and Challenges

_____

_____

_____

_____

Additional Thoughts?

_____

_____

_____

_____

Heaven gives us hope
and makes our present
burdens easier to bear.
-Billy Graham

_____

_____

_____

_____

"When you are grateful for what you have, what you have is more than enough"

⚡ **GRATITUDE** | Today, I am grateful for...

_____

_____

_____

"Feed your soul with God's truth"

⚡ **SCRIPTURE**

1 Timothy 3:3-5
He must not be a heavy drinker or be violent. He must be gentle, not quarrelsome, and not love money. He must manage his own family well, having children who respect and obey him. For if a man cannot manage his own household, how can he take care of God's church?

⚡ **SCRIPTURE**

2 Timothy 2:5-7
And athletes cannot win the prize unless they follow the rules. And hardworking farmers should be the first to enjoy the fruit of their labor. Think about what I am saying. The Lord will help you understand all these things.

What is the Lord speaking into your life through these verses?

_____

_____

What did you learn about the Lord?

_____

_____

"For whom, what and why am I praying today?"

⚡ **Prayer |** Who am I burdened for today?

Who? _____ Why? _____

Who? _____ Why? _____

Who? _____ Why? _____

What? _____

What? _____

Praise: _____

⚡ **Prayer |** What else needs prayer?

_____

_____

_____

⚡ **Answered Prayer |** A good time for graditude

_____

_____

_____

_____

_____

"Capture the essence of the last 24 hours"

⚡ **Journal** | What lessons did I learn?

_____

_____

_____

_____

⚡ **Journal** | Today will be successful if...

_____

_____

_____

_____

⚡ **Journal** | Declaration: Today I will...

_____

_____

_____

_____

PASTOR'S BOOK CLUB
PURPOSEFUL, MEANINGFUL READS
from Pastor Chuck Allen
achuckallen.com

⚡ **Journal** | Things I'm excited about

_____

_____

_____

_____

⚡ **Journal** | Yesterday's Wins and Challenges

_____

_____

_____

_____

Additional Thoughts?

_____

_____

_____

_____

The most eloquent prayer
is the prayer through hands
that heal and bless.
-Billy Graham

_____

_____

_____

_____

"When you are grateful for what you have, what you have is more than enough"

⚡ **GRATITUDE** | Today, I am grateful for...

_____

_____

_____

"Feed your soul with God's truth"

⚡ **SCRIPTURE**

1 Timothy 3:6-7
A church leader must not be a new believer, because he might become proud, and the devil would cause him to fall. Also, people outside the church must speak well of him so that he will not be disgraced and fall into the devil's trap.

⚡ **SCRIPTURE**

2 Timothy 2:8-9
Always remember that Jesus Christ, a descendant of King David, was raised from the dead. This is the Good News I preach. And because I preach this Good News, I am suffering and have been chained like a criminal. But the word of God cannot be chained.

What is the Lord speaking into your life through these verses?

_____

_____

What did you learn about the Lord?

_____

_____

"For whom, what and why am I praying today?"

⚡ **Prayer |** Who am I burdened for today?

Who? _____ Why? _____

Who? _____ Why? _____

Who? _____ Why? _____

What? _____

What? _____

Praise: _____

⚡ **Prayer |** What else needs prayer?

_____

_____

_____

⚡ **Answered Prayer |** A good time for gratitude

_____

_____

_____

_____

_____

"Capture the essence of the last 24 hours"

⚡ **Journal** | What lessons did I learn?

_____

_____

_____

_____

⚡ **Journal** | Today will be successful if...

_____

_____

_____

_____

⚡ **Journal** | Declaration: Today I will...

_____

_____

_____

_____

**WANT TO FILL YOUR DAY WITH
A CUP OF ENCOURAGEMENT?**
Experience the Weekday Podcast
WeekdayPodcast.com
5 minutes a day and 5 days a week

⚡ Journal | Things I'm excited about

_____

_____

_____

_____

⚡ Journal | Yesterday's Wins and Challenges

_____

_____

_____

_____

Additional Thoughts?

_____

_____

_____

_____

Only God who made us can
touch us and change us
and save us from ourselves.
-Billy Graham

_____

_____

_____

_____

_____

_____

"When you are grateful for what you have, what you have is more than enough"

⚡ **GRATITUDE** | Today, I am grateful for...

_____

_____

_____

"Feed your soul with God's truth"

⚡ **SCRIPTURE**

1 Timothy 3:14-16
I am writing these things to you now, even though I hope to be with you soon, so that if I am delayed, you will know how people must conduct themselves in the household of God. This is the church of the living God, which is the pillar and foundation of the truth. Without question, this is the great mystery of our faith: Christ was revealed in a human body and vindicated by the Spirit. He was seen by angels and announced to the nations. He was believed in throughout the world and taken to heaven in glory.

⚡ **SCRIPTURE**

2 Timothy 2:10-11
So I am willing to endure anything if it will bring salvation and eternal glory in Christ Jesus to those God has chosen. This is a trustworthy saying: If we die with him, we will also live with him.

What is the Lord speaking into your life through these verses?

_____

_____

What did you learn about the Lord?

_____

_____

*"For whom, what and why am
I praying today?"*

⚡ **Prayer |** Who am I burdened for today?

Who? _____ Why? _____

Who? _____ Why? _____

Who? _____ Why? _____

What? _____

What? _____

Praise: _____

⚡ **Prayer |** What else needs prayer?

_____

_____

_____

⚡ **Answered Prayer |** A good time for graditude

_____

_____

_____

_____

_____

"Capture the essence of the last 24 hours"

⚡ **Journal** | What lessons did I learn?

_____

_____

_____

_____

⚡ **Journal** | Today will be successful if...

_____

_____

_____

_____

⚡ **Journal** | Declaration: Today I will...

_____

_____

_____

_____

WEEKDAY MEDITATION

Discover Peace, Power, & Direction
ON THE WEEKDAY MEDITATION
Meditative prayer guided by Pastor Chuck Allen
WeekdayMeditation.com

⚡ **Journal** | Things I'm excited about

_____

_____

_____

_____

⚡ **Journal** | Yesterday's Wins and Challenges

_____

_____

_____

_____

Additional Thoughts?

_____

_____

_____

_____

_____   Believers, look up - take
                                  courage. The angels are
_____   nearer than you think.
                                  -Billy Graham
_____

_____

_____

"When you are grateful for what you have, what you have is more than enough"

⚡ **GRATITUDE** | Today, I am grateful for...

_____

_____

_____

"Feed your soul with God's truth"

⚡ **SCRIPTURE**

1 Timothy 4:1-5
Now the Holy Spirit tells us clearly that in the last times some will turn away from the true faith; they will follow deceptive spirits and teachings that come from demons. These people are hypocrites and liars, and their consciences are dead. They will say it is wrong to be married and wrong to eat certain foods. But God created those foods to be eaten with thanks by faithful people who know the truth. Since everything God created is good, we should not reject any of it but receive it with thanks. For we know it is made acceptable by the word of God and prayer.

⚡ **SCRIPTURE**

2 Timothy 2:12-13
If we endure hardship, we will reign with him. If we deny him, he will deny us. If we are unfaithful, he remains faithful, for he cannot deny who he is. Remind everyone about these things, and command them in God's presence to stop fighting over words. Such arguments are useless, and they can ruin those who hear them.

What is the Lord speaking into your life through these verses?

_____

_____

What did you learn about the Lord?

_____

_____

"For whom, what and why am I praying today?"

⚡ **Prayer |** Who am I burdened for today?

Who? _____   Why? _____

Who? _____   Why? _____

Who? _____   Why? _____

What? _____

What? _____

Praise: _____

⚡ **Prayer |** What else needs prayer?

_____

_____

_____

⚡ **Answered Prayer |** A good time for graditude

_____

_____

_____

_____

_____

"Capture the essence of the last 24 hours"

⚡ **Journal** | What lessons did I learn?

_____

_____

_____

_____

⚡ **Journal** | Today will be successful if...

_____

_____

_____

_____

⚡ **Journal** | Declaration: Today I will...

_____

_____

_____

_____

4ForFriday
Recommended Reads, Listens, Learnings,
and Reviews every Friday
from achuckallen.com

⚡ Journal | Things I'm excited about

_____

_____

_____

_____

⚡ Journal | Yesterday's Wins and Challenges

_____

_____

_____

_____

Additional Thoughts?

_____

_____

_____

_____

_____

_____

_____

_____

_____

_____

Every day is a gift from
God, no matter how
old we are.
-Billy Graham

"When you are grateful for what you have, what you have is more than enough"

⚡ **GRATITUDE** | Today, I am grateful for...

_____

_____

_____

"Feed your soul with God's truth"

⚡ **SCRIPTURE**

1 Timothy 4:6-7
f you explain these things to the brothers and sisters,
Timothy, you will be a worthy servant of Christ Jesus,
one who is nourished by the message of faith and
the good teaching you have followed. Do not waste
time arguing over godless ideas and old wives' tales.
Instead, train yourself to be godly.

⚡ **SCRIPTURE**

2 Timothy 2:15-18
Work hard so you can present yourself to God and receive
his approval. Be a good worker, one who does not need
to be ashamed and who correctly explains the word of
truth. Avoid worthless, foolish talk that only leads to more
godless behavior. This kind of talk spreads like cancer, as
in the case of Hymenaeus and Philetus. They have left the
path of truth, claiming that the resurrection of the dead
has already occurred; in this way, they have turned some
people away from the faith.

What is the Lord speaking into your life through these verses?

_____

_____

What did you learn about the Lord?

_____

_____

64

"For whom, what and why am I praying today?"

⚡ **Prayer** | Who am I burdened for today?

Who? _____ Why? _____

Who? _____ Why? _____

Who? _____ Why? _____

What? _____

What? _____

Praise: _____

⚡ **Prayer** | What else needs prayer?

_____

_____

_____

⚡ **Answered Prayer** | A good time for graditude

_____

_____

_____

_____

_____

"Capture the essence of the last 24 hours"

⚡ **Journal |** What lessons did I learn?

_____

_____

_____

_____

⚡ **Journal |** Today will be successful if...

_____

_____

_____

_____

⚡ **Journal |** Declaration: Today I will...

_____

_____

_____

_____

INSTIGATING BETTER BLOG
FRESH THOUGHTS ON
LIFE AND LEADERSHIP
at achuckallen.com

⚡ **Journal** | Things I'm excited about

_____

_____

_____

_____

⚡ **Journal** | Yesterday's Wins and Challenges

_____

_____

_____

_____

Additional Thoughts?

_____

_____

_____

_____   Only the supernatural
                                   love of God through
_____   changed lives can solve
                                   the problems that we
_____   face in our world.
                                   -Billy Graham
_____

_____

_____

*"When you are grateful for what you have,
what you have is more than enough"*

⚡ **GRATITUDE** | Today, I am grateful for...

_____

_____

_____

"Feed your soul with God's truth"

⚡ **SCRIPTURE**

1 Timothy 4:8-10
"Physical training is good, but training for godliness is much better, promising benefits in this life and in the life to come." This is a trustworthy saying, and everyone should accept it. This is why we work hard and continue to struggle, for our hope is in the living God, who is the Savior of all people and particularly of all believers.

⚡ **SCRIPTURE**

2 Timothy 2:19
But God's truth stands firm like a foundation stone with this inscription: "The Lord knows those who are his," and "All who belong to the Lord must turn away from evil."

What is the Lord speaking into your life through these verses?

_____

_____

What did you learn about the Lord?

_____

_____

"For whom, what and why am I praying today?"

⚡ **Prayer |** Who am I burdened for today?

Who? _____ Why? _____

Who? _____ Why? _____

Who? _____ Why? _____

What? _____

What? _____

Praise: _____

⚡ **Prayer |** What else needs prayer?

_____

_____

_____

⚡ **Answered Prayer |** A good time for graditude

_____

_____

_____

_____

_____

⚡ **Journal** | What lessons did I learn?

_____

_____

_____

_____

⚡ **Journal** | Today will be successful if...

_____

_____

_____

_____

⚡ **Journal** | Declaration: Today I will...

_____

_____

_____

_____

PASTOR'S BOOK CLUB
PURPOSEFUL, MEANINGFUL READS
from Pastor Chuck Allen
achuckallen.com

⚡ **Journal** | Things I'm excited about

_____

_____

_____

_____

⚡ **Journal** | Yesterday's Wins and Challenges

_____

_____

_____

_____

Additional Thoughts?

_____

_____

_____

_____

_____

⌐ God is more interested
in your future and your
relationships than you are.
-Billy Graham ⌐

_____

_____

_____

_____

"When you are grateful for what you have, what you have is more than enough"

⚡ **GRATITUDE** | Today, I am grateful for...

_____

_____

_____

"Feed your soul with God's truth"

⚡ **SCRIPTURE**

1 Timothy 4:11-13
Teach these things and insist that everyone learn them. Don't let anyone think less of you because you are young. Be an example to all believers in what you say, in the way you live, in your love, your faith, and your purity. Until I get there, focus on reading the Scriptures to the church, encouraging the believers, and teaching them.

⚡ **SCRIPTURE**

2 Timothy 2:20-21
In a wealthy home some utensils are made of gold and silver, and some are made of wood and clay. The expensive utensils are used for special occasions, and the cheap ones are for everyday use. If you keep yourself pure, you will be a special utensil for honorable use. Your life will be clean, and you will be ready for the Master to use you for every good work.

What is the Lord speaking into your life through these verses?

_____

_____

What did you learn about the Lord?

_____

_____

*"For whom, what and why am
I praying today?"*

⚡ **Prayer |** Who am I burdened for today?

Who? _____   Why? _____

Who? _____   Why? _____

Who? _____   Why? _____

What? _____

What? _____

Praise: _____

⚡ **Prayer |** What else needs prayer?

_____

_____

_____

⚡ **Answered Prayer |** A good time for graditude

_____

_____

_____

_____

_____

"Capture the essence of the last 24 hours"

⚡ **Journal** | What lessons did I learn?

_____

_____

_____

_____

⚡ **Journal** | Today will be successful if...

_____

_____

_____

_____

⚡ **Journal** | Declaration: Today I will...

_____

_____

_____

_____

**WANT TO FILL YOUR DAY WITH
A CUP OF ENCOURAGEMENT?**
Experience the Weekday Podcast
WeekdayPodcast.com
5 minutes a day and 5 days a week

⚡ Journal | Things I'm excited about

_____

_____

_____

_____

⚡ Journal | Yesterday's Wins and Challenges

_____

_____

_____

_____

Additional Thoughts?

_____

_____

_____

_____

_____

Man is not born to atheism.
He is born to believe.
-Billy Graham

_____

_____

_____

_____

*"When you are grateful for what you have,
what you have is more than enough"*

⚡ **GRATITUDE** | Today, I am grateful for...

_____

_____

_____

"Feed your soul with God's truth"

⚡ **SCRIPTURE**

1 Timothy 4:14-16

*Do not neglect the spiritual gift you received through
the prophecy spoken over you when the elders of the
church laid their hands on you. Give your complete
attention to these matters. Throw yourself into your
tasks so that everyone will see your progress. Keep
a close watch on how you live and on your teaching.
Stay true to what is right for the sake of your own
salvation and the salvation of those who hear you.*

⚡ **SCRIPTURE**

2 Timothy 2:22-24

*Run from anything that stimulates youthful lusts. Instead,
pursue righteous living, faithfulness, love, and peace.
Enjoy the companionship of those who call on the Lord
with pure hearts. Again I say, don't get involved in foolish,
ignorant arguments that only start fights. A servant of the
Lord must not quarrel but must be kind to everyone, be
able to teach, and be patient with difficult people.*

What is the Lord speaking into your life through these verses?

_____

_____

What did you learn about the Lord?

_____

_____

"For whom, what and why am I praying today?"

⚡ **Prayer |** Who am I burdened for today?

Who? _____ Why? _____

Who? _____ Why? _____

Who? _____ Why? _____

What? _____

What? _____

Praise: _____

⚡ **Prayer |** What else needs prayer?

_____

_____

_____

⚡ **Answered Prayer |** A good time for gratitude

_____

_____

_____

_____

_____

"Capture the essence of the last 24 hours"

⚡ **Journal** | What lessons did I learn?

_____

_____

_____

_____

⚡ **Journal** | Today will be successful if...

_____

_____

_____

_____

⚡ **Journal** | Declaration: Today I will...

_____

_____

_____

_____

WEEKDAY MEDITATION

Discover Peace, Power, & Direction
ON THE WEEKDAY MEDITATION
Meditative prayer guided by Pastor Chuck Allen
WeekdayMeditation.com

⚡ **Journal** | Things I'm excited about

_____

_____

_____

_____

⚡ **Journal** | Yesterday's Wins and Challenges

_____

_____

_____

_____

Additional Thoughts?

_____

_____

_____

_____

_____

_____

_____

_____

_____

The older I get, the
more important the
eternal becomes
to me personally.
-Billy Graham

"When you are grateful for what you have, what you have is more than enough"

⚡ **GRATITUDE** | Today, I am grateful for...

_____

_____

_____

"Feed your soul with God's truth"

⚡ **SCRIPTURE**

1 Timothy 5:1-2
Never speak harshly to an older man, but appeal to him respectfully as you would to your own father. Talk to younger men as you would to your own brothers. Treat older women as you would your mother, and treat younger women with all purity as you would your own sisters.

⚡ **SCRIPTURE**

2 Timothy 3:1-5
You should know this, Timothy, that in the last days there will be very difficult times. For people will love only themselves and their money. They will be boastful and proud, scoffing at God, disobedient to their parents, and ungrateful. They will consider nothing sacred. They will be unloving and unforgiving; they will slander others and have no self-control. They will be cruel and hate what is good. They will betray their friends, be reckless, be puffed up with pride, and love pleasure rather than God. They will act religious, but they will reject the power that could make them godly. Stay away from people like that!

What is the Lord speaking into your life through these verses?

_____

_____

What did you learn about the Lord?

_____

_____

"For whom, what and why am I praying today?"

⚡ **Prayer** | Who am I burdened for today?

Who? _____ Why? _____

Who? _____ Why? _____

Who? _____ Why? _____

What? _____

What? _____

Praise: _____

⚡ **Prayer** | What else needs prayer?

_____

_____

_____

⚡ **Answered Prayer** | A good time for gratitude

_____

_____

_____ _____

_____

_____

⚡ **Journal** | What lessons did I learn?

_____

_____

_____

_____

⚡ **Journal** | Today will be successful if...

_____

_____

_____

_____

⚡ **Journal** | Declaration: Today I will...

_____

_____

_____

_____

4ForFriday
Recommended Reads, Listens, Learnings,
and Reviews every Friday
from achuckallen.com

⚡ **Journal** | Things I'm excited about

_____

_____

_____

_____

⚡ **Journal** | Yesterday's Wins and Challenges

_____

_____

_____

_____

Additional Thoughts?

_____

_____

_____

_____

_____

_____

_____

_____

_____

_____

⌐ Christ was God in
human flesh, and He
proved it by rising
from the dead.
-Billy Graham ⌐

"When you are grateful for what you have, what you have is more than enough"

⚡ GRATITUDE | Today, I am grateful for...

_____

_____

_____

"Feed your soul with God's truth"

⚡ SCRIPTURE

1 Timothy 5:3-5
Take care of any widow who has no one else to care for her. But if she has children or grandchildren, their first responsibility is to show godliness at home and repay their parents by taking care of them. This is something that pleases God. Now a true widow, a woman who is truly alone in this world, has placed her hope in God. She prays night and day, asking God for his help.

⚡ SCRIPTURE

2 Timothy 3:6-9
They are the kind who work their way into people's homes and win the confidence of vulnerable women who are burdened with the guilt of sin and controlled by various desires. (Such women are forever following new teachings, but they are never able to understand the truth.) These teachers oppose the truth just as Jannes and Jambres opposed Moses. They have depraved minds and a counterfeit faith. But they won't get away with this for long. Someday everyone will recognize what fools they are, just as with Jannes and Jambres.

What is the Lord speaking into your life through these verses?

_____

_____

What did you learn about the Lord?

_____

_____

"For whom, what and why am I praying today?"

⚡ **Prayer |** Who am I burdened for today?

Who? _____ Why? _____

Who? _____ Why? _____

Who? _____ Why? _____

What? _____

What? _____

Praise: _____

⚡ **Prayer |** What else needs prayer?

_____

_____

_____

⚡ **Answered Prayer |** A good time for graditude

_____

_____

_____

_____

_____

"Capture the essence of the last 24 hours"

⚡ **Journal** | What lessons did I learn?

_____

_____

_____

_____

⚡ **Journal** | Today will be successful if...

_____

_____

_____

_____

⚡ **Journal** | Declaration: Today I will...

_____

_____

_____

_____

INSTIGATING BETTER BLOG
FRESH THOUGHTS ON
LIFE AND LEADERSHIP
at achuckallen.com

⚡ Journal | Things I'm excited about

_____

_____

_____

_____

⚡ Journal | Yesterday's Wins and Challenges

_____

_____

_____

_____

Additional Thoughts?

_____

_____

_____

_____

_____

God has given us two
hands - one to receive
with and the other to give
with. We are not cisterns
made for hoarding; we are
channels made for sharing.
-Billy Graham

_____

_____

_____

_____

"When you are grateful for what you have, what you have is more than enough"

⚡ **GRATITUDE** | Today, I am grateful for...

_____

_____

_____

"Feed your soul with God's truth"

⚡ **SCRIPTURE**

1 Timothy 5:17-18
Elders who do their work well should be respected and paid well, especially those who work hard at both preaching and teaching. For the Scripture says, "You must not muzzle an ox to keep it from eating as it treads out the grain." And in another place, "Those who work deserve their pay!"

⚡ **SCRIPTURE**

2 Timothy 3:10-13
But you, Timothy, certainly know what I teach, and how I live, and what my purpose in life is. You know my faith, my patience, my love, and my endurance. You know how much persecution and suffering I have endured. You know all about how I was persecuted in Antioch, Iconium, and Lystra—but the Lord rescued me from all of it. Yes, and everyone who wants to live a godly life in Christ Jesus will suffer persecution. But evil people and impostors will flourish. They will deceive others and will themselves be deceived.

What is the Lord speaking into your life through these verses?

_____

_____

What did you learn about the Lord?

_____

_____

"For whom, what and why am I praying today?"

⚡ **Prayer |** Who am I burdened for today?

Who? _____ Why? _____

Who? _____ Why? _____

Who? _____ Why? _____

What? _____

What? _____

Praise: _____

⚡ **Prayer |** What else needs prayer?

_____

_____

_____

⚡ **Answered Prayer |** A good time for graditude

_____

_____

_____

_____

_____

⚡ **Journal** | What lessons did I learn?

_____

_____

_____

_____

⚡ **Journal** | Today will be successful if...

_____

_____

_____

_____

⚡ **Journal** | Declaration: Today I will...

_____

_____

_____

_____

PASTOR'S BOOK CLUB
PURPOSEFUL, MEANINGFUL READS
from Pastor Chuck Allen
achuckallen.com

⚡ Journal | Things I'm excited about

_____

_____

_____

_____

⚡ Journal | Yesterday's Wins and Challenges

_____

_____

_____

_____

Additional Thoughts?

_____

_____

_____

_____

_____

The moment we take our
last breath on earth, we
take our first in heaven.
-Billy Graham

_____

_____

_____

_____

"When you are grateful for what you have,
what you have is more than enough"

⚡ **GRATITUDE** | Today, I am grateful for...

_____

_____

_____

"Feed your soul with God's truth"

⚡ **SCRIPTURE**

1 Timothy 5:21-22
I solemnly command you in the presence of
God and Christ Jesus and the highest angels
to obey these instructions without taking sides
or showing favoritism to anyone. Never be in a
hurry about appointing a church leader. Do not
share in the sins of others. Keep yourself pure.

⚡ **SCRIPTURE**

2 Timothy 3:14-15
But you must remain faithful to the things you have
been taught. You know they are true, for you know you
can trust those who taught you. You have been taught
the holy Scriptures from childhood, and they have
given you the wisdom to receive the salvation that
comes by trusting in Christ Jesus.

What is the Lord speaking into your life through these verses?

_____

_____

What did you learn about the Lord?

_____

_____

"For whom, what and why am I praying today?"

⚡ **Prayer** | Who am I burdened for today?

Who? _____ Why? _____

Who? _____ Why? _____

Who? _____ Why? _____

What? _____

What? _____

Praise: _____

⚡ **Prayer** | What else needs prayer?

_____

_____

_____

⚡ **Answered Prayer** | A good time for graditude

_____

_____

_____

_____

_____

Journal | What lessons did I learn?

_____

_____

_____

_____

Journal | Today will be successful if...

_____

_____

_____

_____

Journal | Declaration: Today I will...

_____

_____

_____

_____

**WANT TO FILL YOUR DAY WITH
A CUP OF ENCOURAGEMENT?**
Experience the Weekday Podcast
WeekdayPodcast.com
5 minutes a day and 5 days a week

⚡ **Journal** | Things I'm excited about

_____

_____

_____

_____

⚡ **Journal** | Yesterday's Wins and Challenges

_____

_____

_____

_____

Additional Thoughts?

_____

_____

_____

_____

_____
⌐
  The only hope for
enduring peace is
Jesus Christ.
-Billy Graham
     ⌐

_____

_____

_____

_____

*"When you are grateful for what you have,
what you have is more than enough"*

⚡ **GRATITUDE** | Today, I am grateful for...

_____

_____

_____

"Feed your soul with God's truth"

⚡ **SCRIPTURE**

1 Timothy 5:24-25
*Remember, the sins of some people are obvious, leading
them to certain judgment. But there are others whose
sins will not be revealed until later. In the same way, the
good deeds of some people are obvious. And the good
deeds done in secret will someday come to light.*

⚡ **SCRIPTURE**

2 Timothy 3:16-17
*All Scripture is inspired by God and is useful to teach
us what is true and to make us realize what is wrong
in our lives. It corrects us when we are wrong and
teaches us to do what is right. God uses it to prepare
and equip his people to do every good work.*

What is the Lord speaking into your life through these verses?

_____

_____

What did you learn about the Lord?

_____

_____

"For whom, what and why am I praying today?"

⚡ **Prayer** | Who am I burdened for today?

Who? _____ Why? _____

Who? _____ Why? _____

Who? _____ Why? _____

What? _____

What? _____

Praise: _____

⚡ **Prayer** | What else needs prayer?

_____

_____

_____

⚡ **Answered Prayer** | A good time for gratitude

_____

_____

_____

_____

_____

⚡ **Journal** | What lessons did I learn?

_____

_____

_____

_____

⚡ **Journal** | Today will be successful if...

_____

_____

_____

_____

⚡ **Journal** | Declaration: Today I will...

_____

_____

_____

_____

WEEKDAY
MEDITATION

Discover Peace, Power, & Direction
ON THE WEEKDAY MEDITATION
Meditative prayer guided by Pastor Chuck Allen
WeekdayMeditation.com

⚡ Journal | Things I'm excited about

_____

_____

_____

_____

⚡ Journal | Yesterday's Wins and Challenges

_____

_____

_____

_____

Additional Thoughts?

_____

_____

_____

_____

_____

The cross shows us the
seriousness of our sin—
but it also shows us the
immeasurable love of God.
-Billy Graham

_____

_____

_____

_____

_____

"When you are grateful for what you have, what you have is more than enough"

⚡ **GRATITUDE** | Today, I am grateful for...

_____

_____

_____

"Feed your soul with God's truth"

⚡ **SCRIPTURE**

1 Timothy 6:3-5
Some people may contradict our teaching, but these are the wholesome teachings of the Lord Jesus Christ. These teachings promote a godly life. Anyone who teaches something different is arrogant and lacks understanding. Such a person has an unhealthy desire to quibble over the meaning of words. This stirs up arguments ending in jealousy, division, slander, and evil suspicions. These people always cause trouble. Their minds are corrupt, and they have turned their backs on the truth. To them, a show of godliness is just a way to become wealthy.

⚡ **SCRIPTURE**

2 Timothy 4:1-2
I solemnly urge you in the presence of God and Christ Jesus, who will someday judge the living and the dead when he comes to set up his Kingdom: Preach the word of God. Be prepared, whether the time is favorable or not. Patiently correct, rebuke, and encourage your people with good teaching.

What is the Lord speaking into your life through these verses?

_____

_____

What did you learn about the Lord?

_____

_____

"For whom, what and why am I praying today?"

⚡ **Prayer** | Who am I burdened for today?

Who? _____ Why? _____

Who? _____ Why? _____

Who? _____ Why? _____

What? _____

What? _____

Praise: _____

⚡ **Prayer** | What else needs prayer?

_____

_____

_____

⚡ **Answered Prayer** | A good time for gratitude

_____

_____

_____

_____

_____

"Capture the essence of the last 24 hours"

⚡ **Journal** | What lessons did I learn?

_____

_____

_____

_____

⚡ **Journal** | Today will be successful if...

_____

_____

_____

_____

⚡ **Journal** | Declaration: Today I will...

_____

_____

_____

_____

4ForFriday
Recommended Reads, Listens, Learnings,
and Reviews every Friday
from achuckallen.com

⚡ Journal | Things I'm excited about

_____

_____

_____

_____

⚡ Journal | Yesterday's Wins and Challenges

_____

_____

_____

_____

Additional Thoughts?

_____

_____

_____

_____

_____

Take one day at a time.
Today, after all, is the
tomorrow you worried
about yesterday.
-Billy Graham

_____

_____

_____

_____

_____

*"When you are grateful for what you have,
what you have is more than enough"*

⚡ **GRATITUDE** | Today, I am grateful for...

_____

_____

_____

"Feed your soul with God's truth"

⚡ **SCRIPTURE**

1 Timothy 6:6-8
*Yet true godliness with contentment is itself great
wealth. After all, we brought nothing with us when
we came into the world, and we can't take anything
with us when we leave it. So if we have enough food
and clothing, let us be content.*

⚡ **SCRIPTURE**

2 Timothy 4:3-5
*For a time is coming when people will no longer listen to
sound and wholesome teaching. They will follow their
own desires and will look for teachers who will tell them
whatever their itching ears want to hear. They will reject
the truth and chase after myths. But you should keep a
clear mind in every situation. Don't be afraid of suffering
for the Lord. Work at telling others the Good News, and
fully carry out the ministry God has given you.*

What is the Lord speaking into your life through these verses?

_____

_____

What did you learn about the Lord?

_____

_____

"For whom, what and why am I praying today?"

⚡ **Prayer |** Who am I burdened for today?

Who? _____ Why? _____

Who? _____ Why? _____

Who? _____ Why? _____

What? _____

What? _____

Praise: _____

⚡ **Prayer |** What else needs prayer?

_____

_____

_____

⚡ **Answered Prayer |** A good time for graditude

_____

_____

_____

_____

_____

⚡ **Journal** | What lessons did I learn?

_____

_____

_____

_____

⚡ **Journal** | Today will be successful if...

_____

_____

_____

_____

⚡ **Journal** | Declaration: Today I will...

_____

_____

_____

_____

INSTIGATING BETTER BLOG
FRESH THOUGHTS ON
LIFE AND LEADERSHIP
at achuckallen.com

Journal | Things I'm excited about

_____

_____

_____

_____

Journal | Yesterday's Wins and Challenges

_____

_____

_____

_____

Additional Thoughts?

_____

_____

_____

_____

_____

The will of God will not
take us where the grace
of God cannot sustain us.
-Billy Graham

_____

_____

_____

_____

*"When you are grateful for what you have,
what you have is more than enough"*

⚡ **GRATITUDE** | Today, I am grateful for...

_____

_____

_____

"Feed your soul with God's truth"

⚡ **SCRIPTURE**

1 Timothy 6:9-10
*But people who long to be rich fall into temptation and
are trapped by many foolish and harmful desires that
plunge them into ruin and destruction. For the love of
money is the root of all kinds of evil. And some people,
craving money, have wandered from the true faith and
pierced themselves with many sorrows.*

⚡ **SCRIPTURE**

2 Timothy 4:6-8
*As for me, my life has already been poured out as an
offering to God. The time of my death is near. I have
fought the good fight, I have finished the race, and
I have remained faithful. And now the prize awaits
me—the crown of righteousness, which the Lord, the
righteous Judge, will give me on the day of his return.
And the prize is not just for me but for all who eagerly
look forward to his appearing.*

What is the Lord speaking into your life through these verses?

_____

_____

What did you learn about the Lord?

_____

_____

"For whom, what and why am I praying today?"

⚡ **Prayer |** Who am I burdened for today?

Who? _____ Why? _____

Who? _____ Why? _____

Who? _____ Why? _____

What? _____

What? _____

Praise: _____

⚡ **Prayer |** What else needs prayer?

_____

_____

_____

⚡ **Answered Prayer |** A good time for gratitude

_____

_____

_____

_____

_____

⚡ Journal | What lessons did I learn?

_____

_____

_____

_____

⚡ Journal | Today will be successful if...

_____

_____

_____

_____

⚡ Journal | Declaration: Today I will...

_____

_____

_____

_____

PASTOR'S BOOK CLUB
PURPOSEFUL, MEANINGFUL READS
from Pastor Chuck Allen
achuckallen.com

⚡ Journal | Things I'm excited about

_____

_____

_____

_____

⚡ Journal | Yesterday's Wins and Challenges

_____

_____

_____

_____

Additional Thoughts?

_____

_____

_____

_____

_____

_____

_____

_____

_____

_____

There is nothing wrong
with men possessing
riches. The wrong comes
when riches possess men.
-Billy Graham

"When you are grateful for what you have, what you have is more than enough"

⚡ **GRATITUDE** | Today, I am grateful for...

_____

_____

_____

"Feed your soul with God's truth"

⚡ **SCRIPTURE**

1 Timothy 6:11-12
But you, Timothy, are a man of God; so run from all these evil things. Pursue righteousness and a godly life, along with faith, love, perseverance, and gentleness. Fight the good fight for the true faith. Hold tightly to the eternal life to which God has called you, which you have declared so well before many witnesses.

⚡ **SCRIPTURE**

2 Timothy 4:9-13
Timothy, please come as soon as you can. Demas has deserted me because he loves the things of this life and has gone to Thessalonica. Crescens has gone to Galatia, and Titus has gone to Dalmatia. Only Luke is with me. Bring Mark with you when you come, for he will be helpful to me in my ministry. I sent Tychicus to Ephesus. When you come, be sure to bring the coat I left with Carpus at Troas. Also bring my books, and especially my papers.

What is the Lord speaking into your life through these verses?

_____

_____

What did you learn about the Lord?

_____

_____

"For whom, what and why am I praying today?"

⚡ **Prayer** | Who am I burdened for today?

Who? _____   Why? _____

Who? _____   Why? _____

Who? _____   Why? _____

What? _____

What? _____

Praise: _____

⚡ **Prayer** | What else needs prayer?

_____

_____

_____

⚡ **Answered Prayer** | A good time for gratitude

_____

_____

_____

_____

_____

"Capture the essence of the last 24 hours"

⚡ **Journal** | What lessons did I learn?

_____

_____

_____

_____

⚡ **Journal** | Today will be successful if...

_____

_____

_____

_____

⚡ **Journal** | Declaration: Today I will...

_____

_____

_____

_____

**WANT TO FILL YOUR DAY WITH
A CUP OF ENCOURAGEMENT?**
Experience the Weekday Podcast
WeekdayPodcast.com
5 minutes a day and 5 days a week

⚡ Journal | Things I'm excited about

_____

_____

_____

_____

⚡ Journal | Yesterday's Wins and Challenges

_____

_____

_____

_____

Additional Thoughts?

_____

_____

_____

_____

_____

_____

_____

_____

_____

Knowing we will be with
Christ forever far outweighs
our burdens today! Keep
your eyes on eternity!
-Billy Graham

*"When you are grateful for what you have,
what you have is more than enough"*

⚡ **GRATITUDE** | Today, I am grateful for...

_____

_____

_____

"Feed your soul with God's truth"

⚡ **SCRIPTURE**

1 Timothy 6:13-14
*And I charge you before God, who gives life to all, and
before Christ Jesus, who gave a good testimony before
Pontius Pilate, that you obey this command without
wavering. Then no one can find fault with you from
now until our Lord Jesus Christ comes again.*

⚡ **SCRIPTURE**

2 Timothy 4:14-15
*Alexander the coppersmith did me much harm, but the
Lord will judge him for what he has done. Be careful of
him, for he fought against everything we said.*

What is the Lord speaking into your life through these verses?

_____

_____

What did you learn about the Lord?

_____

_____

"For whom, what and why am I praying today?"

⚡ **Prayer** | Who am I burdened for today?

Who? _____ Why? _____

Who? _____ Why? _____

Who? _____ Why? _____

What? _____

What? _____

Praise: _____

⚡ **Prayer** | What else needs prayer?

_____

_____

_____

⚡ **Answered Prayer** | A good time for graditude

_____

_____

_____

_____

_____

"Capture the essence of the last 24 hours"

⚡ **Journal |** What lessons did I learn?

_____

_____

_____

_____

⚡ **Journal |** Today will be successful if...

_____

_____

_____

_____

⚡ **Journal |** Declaration: Today I will...

_____

_____

_____

_____

WEEKDAY MEDITATION

Discover Peace, Power, & Direction
ON THE WEEKDAY MEDITATION
Meditative prayer guided by Pastor Chuck Allen
WeekdayMeditation.com

⚡ Journal | Things I'm excited about

_____

_____

_____

_____

⚡ Journal | Yesterday's Wins and Challenges

_____

_____

_____

_____

Additional Thoughts?

_____

_____

_____

_____

_____

It is the Holy Spirit's job to
convict, God's job to judge
and my job to love.
-Billy Graham

_____

_____

_____

"When you are grateful for what you have, what you have is more than enough"

⚡ **GRATITUDE** | Today, I am grateful for...

_____

_____

_____

"Feed your soul with God's truth"

⚡ **SCRIPTURE**

1 Timothy 4:15-16
For, At just the right time Christ will be revealed from heaven by the blessed and only almighty God, the King of all kings and Lord of all lords. He alone can never die, and he lives in light so brilliant that no human can approach him. No human eye has ever seen him, nor ever will. All honor and power to him forever! Amen.

⚡ **SCRIPTURE**

2 Timothy 4:16-17
The first time I was brought before the judge, no one came with me. Everyone abandoned me. May it not be counted against them. But the Lord stood with me and gave me strength so that I might preach the Good News in its entirety for all the Gentiles to hear. And he rescued me from certain death.

What is the Lord speaking into your life through these verses?

_____

_____

What did you learn about the Lord?

_____

_____

"For whom, what and why am I praying today?"

⚡ **Prayer** | Who am I burdened for today?

Who? _____ Why? _____

Who? _____ Why? _____

Who? _____ Why? _____

What? _____

What? _____

Praise: _____

⚡ **Prayer** | What else needs prayer?

_____

_____

_____

⚡ **Answered Prayer** | A good time for graditude

_____

_____

_____

_____

_____

⚡ **Journal** | What lessons did I learn?

_____

_____

_____

_____

⚡ **Journal** | Today will be successful if...

_____

_____

_____

_____

⚡ **Journal** | Declaration: Today I will...

_____

_____

_____

_____

4ForFriday
Recommended Reads, Listens, Learnings,
and Reviews every Friday
from achuckallen.com

⚡ **Journal** | Things I'm excited about

_____

_____

_____

_____

⚡ **Journal** | Yesterday's Wins and Challenges

_____

_____

_____

_____

Additional Thoughts?

_____

_____

_____

_____

_____

> Sin is the second most
> powerful force in the
> universe, for it sent Jesus
> to the cross. Only one
> force is greater—
> the love of God.
> -Billy Graham

_____

_____

_____

S M T W TH F S

*"When you are grateful for what you have,
what you have is more than enough"*

⚡ **GRATITUDE** | Today, I am grateful for...

_____

_____

_____

"Feed your soul with God's truth"

⚡ **SCRIPTURE**

1 Timothy 6:17-18
*Teach those who are rich in this world not to be proud and
not to trust in their money, which is so unreliable. Their
trust should be in God, who richly gives us all we need for
our enjoyment. Tell them to use their money to do good.
They should be rich in good works and generous to those
in need, always being ready to share with others.*

⚡ **SCRIPTURE**

2 Timothy 4:18
*Yes, and the Lord will deliver me from every evil
attack and will bring me safely into his heavenly
Kingdom. All glory to God forever and ever! Amen.*

What is the Lord speaking into your life through these verses?

_____

_____

What did you learn about the Lord?

_____

_____

"For whom, what and why am I praying today?"

⚡ **Prayer** | Who am I burdened for today?

Who? _____ Why? _____

Who? _____ Why? _____

Who? _____ Why? _____

What? _____

What? _____

Praise: _____

⚡ **Prayer** | What else needs prayer?

_____

_____

_____

⚡ **Answered Prayer** | A good time for gratitude

_____

_____

_____

_____

_____

"Capture the essence of the last 24 hours"

⚡ Journal | What lessons did I learn?

_____

_____

_____

_____

⚡ Journal | Today will be successful if...

_____

_____

_____

_____

⚡ Journal | Declaration: Today I will...

_____

_____

_____

_____

INSTIGATING BETTER BLOG
FRESH THOUGHTS ON
LIFE AND LEADERSHIP
at achuckallen.com

⚡ **Journal** | Things I'm excited about

_____

_____

_____

_____

⚡ **Journal** | Yesterday's Wins and Challenges

_____

_____

_____

_____

Additional Thoughts?

_____

_____

_____

_____

_____

When we come to the
end of ourselves, we
come to the
beginning of God.
-Billy Graham

_____

_____

_____

_____

_____

*"When you are grateful for what you have,
what you have is more than enough"*

⚡ **GRATITUDE** | Today, I am grateful for...

_____

_____

_____

"Feed your soul with God's truth"

⚡ **SCRIPTURE**

1 Timothy 6:19-21
*By doing this they will be storing up their treasure
as a good foundation for the future so that they may
experience true life. Timothy, guard what God has
entrusted to you. Avoid godless, foolish discussions with
those who oppose you with their so-called knowledge.
Some people have wandered from the faith by following
such foolishness. May God's grace be with you all.*

⚡ **SCRIPTURE**

2 Timothy 4:22
*May the Lord be with your spirit. And may
his grace be with all of you.*

What is the Lord speaking into your life through these verses?

_____

_____

What did you learn about the Lord?

_____

_____

"For whom, what and why am I praying today?"

⚡ **Prayer |** Who am I burdened for today?

Who? _____ Why? _____

Who? _____ Why? _____

Who? _____ Why? _____

What? _____

What? _____

Praise: _____

⚡ **Prayer |** What else needs prayer?

_____

_____

_____

⚡ **Answered Prayer |** A good time for gratitude

_____

_____

_____

_____

_____

⚡ **Journal |** What lessons did I learn?

_____

_____

_____

_____

⚡ **Journal |** Today will be successful if...

_____

_____

_____

_____

⚡ **Journal |** Declaration: Today I will...

_____

_____

_____

_____

PASTOR'S BOOK CLUB
PURPOSEFUL, MEANINGFUL READS
from Pastor Chuck Allen
achuckallen.com

⚡ **Journal** | Things I'm excited about

_____

_____

_____

_____

⚡ **Journal** | Yesterday's Wins and Challenges

_____

_____

_____

_____

Additional Thoughts?

_____

_____

_____

_____

_____

_____

We are the Bibles the world
is reading; we are the creeds
the world is needing; we are
the sermons the
world is heeding.
-Billy Graham

_____

_____

_____